May You Be Well

everyday good vibes for the spiritual

For Jennie, my beloved friend
My godsons, Oliver and Daniel
And my dearest Brooke and James
May you all be well.

An Hachette UK Company
www.hachette.co.uk

First published in Great Britain in 2021 by Pyramid,
an imprint of Octopus Publishing Group Ltd
Carmelite House, 50 Victoria Embankment,
London, EC4Y 0DZ
www.octopusbooks.co.uk

Distributed in the US by
Hachette Book Group
1290 Avenue of the Americas
4th and 5th Floors
New York, NY 10104

Distributed in Canada by
Canadian Manda Group
664 Annette St.
Tornoto, Ontario, Canada, M6S 2CB

ISBN 978-07537-3457-5

A CIP catalogue record for this book is available from
the British Library

Printed and bound in China

10 9 8 7 6 5 4 3 2 1

May You Be Well

everyday good vibes for the spiritual

Cheryl Rickman

introduction

When times are tough most of us pray;
not necessarily to a God, but perhaps to
the Universe, or to our higher selves, or
to some cosmic spiritual support system.
Many of us also affirm positive messages
to give us strength, belief and hope.

We ask for guidance and support to
help us through our day, we pray for our
families and friends; that they may be safe
and well, we give blessings for what we
have and pray for what we hope to have –
be it health or happiness or hope.

May You Be Well is a collection of soul-soothing blessings, affirmations and prayers for non-believers, believers in something or someone, and believers in everything or nothing.

Just everyday good vibes for health, happiness and hope.

positive emotions

on gratitude

Thank you. Thank you.

I am blessed.

No matter what challenges and difficulties come my way, I still have so much to be grateful for.

So I give thanks for all that I have and all that I will have.

I feel the gratitude rising in my heart, a ball of light flowing round my body.

With the deepest gratitude I savour this moment.

Thank you. Thank you.

I am blessed.

———

a blessing
for gladness

Dear gladness
Wrap me in your joy.

Let me delight in your glory
And share in your story.

And feel your magic
Deep in my heart.

And cherish your warmth
Until next time.

———

a prayer
about hope

The road will bend
The trees will sway
The clouds will pass
The river will flow

The rain will fall
The sun will shine
Trust in the journey
All shall be well.

Even when I cannot see the road ahead, I
will use my hope like a torch so I may take
the first step.

———

an appreciation affirmation

I am here to pay attention
To notice with curiosity
To savour and delight in gladness.

May I find something to be grateful
for, always.

———

a blessing on savouring

Rather than worrying about a future I
cannot see and ruminating on a past
I cannot change, I choose to focus on a
present that I can either enjoy or let
pass me by.

I choose to cherish and savour right now.

I choose to make the most of each moment
that makes up my life.

———

a blessing for ordinary things

May I appreciate the gladness of
a window
The joy of putting pen to paper
The ability to be thankful.

May I appreciate the people here, now, and the ones who came before me.

May I appreciate the slight smile, the tiny tokens
And may I feel gratitude for the ordinary things.

———

a blessing on living

I am living a good life.

I trust in this and in myself.

———

an affirmation
for positivity

I will be the cheer today
I will cheer people up
I will cheer myself on
I will speak for hope and listen to joy and
I shall dance.

The difficulties and challenges count by
showing me how strong I am.

To help express my feelings, I'm popping
that beach ball. The one I keep trying
to push down under water, but keeps on
popping up again. Usually when I'm in the
shower. Or turning the light off to go to
sleep.

So I'm not pushing it down anymore.

Today's the day I pop it and release those

feelings and deal with those emotions and choose expression over suppression.

———

for help with hope

Today may be a struggle
But I know things can get better.

I'll feel the waves wash over my feet and the squelch of sand underfoot
I'll smile at my footprints and watch the bright sunset
I'll sip my tea and eat good cake and belly laugh out loud
I'll hear the birdsong sing to me and walk among the trees.

And when I do, my head will lift from underneath this cloud.

———

resilience

a prayer for resilience

May I wriggle my way out of struggles and help others to do the same.

When worries overwhelm me and stare me in the face, may I banish all blame and shame.

When I come undone and get stuck, may I have faith to do myself back up.

May I remember what I have wrangled with before and use that same compass to navigate my way through it all.

Whatever thorny obstacles block my path, may I emerge the other side with my hands on my hips.

Powerful, taller and stronger.

———

on resilience

Dark defeat, I have known you
Suffering and pain, I have felt you
Loss and struggle, I have seen you
But from the depths I have risen.

And I will again.

Because warmth and care, I see you
Gentle kindness, I hear you
Compassion and love, I feel you
And together, with you, I shall rise.

———

a prayer for coping

When life gets difficult and overwhelming
When I feel out of control
May I remember that this too shall pass.

May I take a deep breath in and out a few times.

May I remember how far I've come and what I've dealt with.

And may I choose to focus on one very small thing that I can count on in this moment.

Like a hot cup of tea to warm me up
Like a hug from someone to cheer me up
Like a walk round the block to lift me up.

Onwards and upwards.

_____

for help
with fear

Dear fear
Oh how you underestimate me.

I'm braver than you think
I've triumphed before
I've been through a lot
I've battled and struggled
I've been knocked down.

And yet I've got up.

So here I'm still standing
And I know I've got this.

———

for help with overwhelming feelings

I don't need to do it all
I can say no sometimes.

I owe it to myself and my mental health
To put things down once in a while
I will get to that which I leave for now.

I'm in charge of what I do and when
So let's undo some of this doing
And leave it until tomorrow
Or the next day
Or never if I choose to rest.

Because I'm in control of me.

———

an affirmation about asking for help

I need not shoulder the days which are tough I can ask for a shoulder to rest on.

I am not a burden and I can ask for help to unburden myself.

I can let kindness in and be a conduit for it.

Let me squeeze the balm of kindness onto me as I have done unto others.

To feel that ripple returning to me.

My heart is open to what the world has to offer.

_____

a blessing of reassurance

I hear you whisper in my ear:

It's okay
It's alright

And I feel that you're right.

———

a poem about doing difficult things

What if I fall?
What if you fly?

What if I forget?
What if you remember?

What if I get it completely wrong?
What if you do well and your heart sings a song?

What if I really embarrass myself?
What if you shine and are proud of yourself?

With all these what-ifs about what might
happen, and no-one knows what, that
much is certain.

Isn't it better to get on and try?

To not let fear stop you, take a chance, see
how high.

———

a prayer
for challenging
times

Tough, teary times shape me
Mountains prepare me.

Let me rise to the challenges ahead of me
And recover and bounce back again.

I believe in myself now
I do.

I'm a survivor and comfort-zone stretcher.

I can, I will, I am, I do.

I'm ready to take life on.

———

relationships
with others

a prayer for choosing love

When I feel misunderstood
I choose love anyway.

When I'm unheard and unseen
I choose love anyway.

When I've been hurt and feel pained
I choose love anyway.

I choose love for my fellow humans.

I choose love for myself.

I choose love for the world.

May we all choose love, even when it feels
easier not to; even when it's easier to choose
judgement or scorn, mistrust and hatred.

Instead, today, I will choose love.

_____

a prayer to heal relationships

May I open my heart more readily
So I can see the person I'm struggling with
in a fresh light.

Let me see them for a moment as their
child selves
Let me look at their innocent or cheeky
face peering up at me.

May I forgive them for whatever they've
said or done.

Let my bitterness fade so we can do
better, together
So we can build bridges as we softly shift
Towards harmony and unity.

May I see those I struggle with through a
lens of understanding

May I bless those I've seen as enemies, the
same as I bless my friends.

May my relationships heal with the salve
of patience.

And in time become strengthened
By the balm of compassion.

———

for peace

Sometimes not saying anything at all
says everything.

———

on grief

I love you
I miss you.

But I know you are here
In my heart
In my memories
In my soul
By my side
Forever with me in spirit
Never forgotten
Always cherished.

With me. Knowing me. Guiding me.

_____

for help with listening

When others share their good news with me

May I remember to ask them to tell me more.

May I help them relive those moments of joy.

May I hear them and delight in the stories
they share.

May I always listen and pay attention to the
good things that happen to those for whom
I care.

_____

a prayer about responding well

I cannot control what others say or do
But I can control my response.

Let me pause in that silence before I react
And choose with wisdom how best to respond.

With compassion
With patience
With empathy
With love.

May I choose wisely
And remember that pausing enhances my
ability to choose more likely.

_____

a blessing of remembrance

I am made of tiny pieces of those I have loved.

Thank you for being in this world with me.

You are still here with each step I take
You give me the strength I need
You return me to my heart
You keep me grounded
You tap me on the shoulder when magic
is near so I don't miss it.

And while I miss you
I feel your love and your legacies all
around me.

_____

a blessing for friendship

Those who see me
I thank you for noticing
and observing and caring.

Those who hear me
I thank you for listening
and asking and checking.

Those who value me
I thank you for appreciating
and loving and feeling
my friendship.

Just as I value yours.

_____

a friendship prayer

I give thanks to my friends.

Just knowing you are there comforts me.

You are my mug of hot tea and hot
buttered toast
You are my glowing log fire and warm
shawl around my shoulders
You are my golden sunrise and expansive
blue sky.

Thank you for being you, and thank you for
being here with me.

———

a prayer for kindness

Who can I reach out to today?
And what should I be sure to say?

Who can I make smile tomorrow?
And how shall I lift them from their sorrow?

Who can I take care of this week?
Perhaps with a hug, cheek to cheek?

I know connection will lift us both up
The beauty of unity fills each cup.

_____

a blessing for unconditional love

May I do more of what makes my eyes
sparkle and my heart sing.

May I encourage others to do so too.

May I spend time with those who make me
laugh heartily
And make me smile willingly
With no need to put on a brave face
Because they can see my real face
My perfectly imperfect face
Which I give the thumbs up to
Just like they do
Unconditionally.

My friends, my family and I.

_____

a blessing for unity

Sisters and misters
Ebbing and flowing
Paper-chain people
Connected
Supporting.

When we hold out our hands
To the left or the right
We will find another
Who's fought the same fight.

It's no surprise
Together we rise.

———

a blessing for strangers

The light in me sees the light in you
The best in me values the best of you
The worst of me seeks to understand the
worst of you.

We are in this together.

May you be well.

May we live with ease.

May you be supported by the warmth
of love.

_____

a blessing about give and take

I've spent so long putting others first
But now it's time to realise
There is room for me to receive help
Whenever I may need it.

I welcome help
I'm open to it
Supportive words and love.

Taking a sip from the cup of care as well
as making cups for others.

I cannot pour from an empty cup
And so today I'll fill it.

———

a loving kindness blessing

May you be safe and happy
May you be peaceful and calm
May you be healthy and strong
May you live with ease and wellbeing
May all beings be well
May everyone experience great joy
May I be safe and happy
May I be peaceful and calm
May I be healthy and strong
May I live with ease and wellbeing
May I accept myself just the way I am.

_____

a prayer for equality

Bless us with compassion to see each
other as equals
To replace judgement with curiosity
To replace scorn with mutual acceptance.

Help us see we were all born equal
With the same foundation of bones
underneath skin
All of us smiling in the same language
Every one of us part of the human race.

We may differ in talent and skill
In circumstances and gender
In skin colour and eye colour
In height and weight
And can shine in our individuality yet unite
in our shared humanity.

In our humanity we are equal.

Bless us with compassion to notice our
shared struggles and respect each other's
beating hearts
To be united together, in this life, on
this planet
Our equal right to be well and do well; to
keep our families safe
Equal in the right to dream our dreams
And achieve what we can with the effort
we put in.

Not dependent on the colour of our skin
May we always respect our equality.

———

a blessing for difficult relationships

May I open my heart more readily
So I can see the true person in front of me
So I may see them in a new light
For with them I don't wish to fight.

Let me put myself in their shoes.

Let me have the compassion and empathy
to be considerate of their point of view.

May I forgive what's been said and done
So my bitterness may fade.

We can do better, together
We can build bridges

And softly waltz
Towards harmony and unity.

May I view them now through a lens
of understanding.

May I bless those I've seen as enemies, the
same as I bless my friends.

May my relationships heal with the salve of
patience and in time become strengthened
By the balm of compassion.

———

a blessing for uniting for a common cause

May I see how much power I have to bring about change.

I may be one person but I can speak for many.

My solitary voice can unite others to join me in my quest.

My solitary action can galvanise others to move alongside me.

Forward we march
Together.

The courage of my convictions can inspire a movement.

Moving together in unison
May our paths be blessed as we
step forward.

One step, then another, to our
desired future.

May we be rewarded for the effort we put in
As our dreams for change come to fruition.

May our journey be worthwhile.

May we celebrate our progress
Knowing each step we take is building a
road towards a future we believe in.

Giving us hope as we progress towards
great possibilities.

Together we will march.

———

achievement and the future

an affirmation of achievement

One tiny step at a time
is an act of devotion.

One tiny step at a time
will spur me towards my destination.

Gradually
Progressing.

And so I take a step forward and onward
One tiny step at a time.

_____

a prayer for self-belief

How might I live my life if I were less afraid?

What might life look like if I took the risk and the plunge and the bull by the horns?

Who might I become if I did rather than didn't?

Because I can, you know, I really can.

And so, perhaps, I will try
Not tomorrow, but today.

I believe in myself.

I can do things which challenge me.

I have done hard things before and I have survived.

I can. Yes I can. And I will.

———

on
unlearning

I have decided to unlearn all the things
that don't serve me.

Like comparing myself to others.
Comparison steals joy and makes me
feel worse than I deserve. So be gone
comparison.

May I instead accept and be satisfied with
being all that I am, including the imperfect
parts, especially the imperfect parts, for
they make me uniquely me.

I am me. There is nobody else who can be
better at being me, than me. That's what
matters most.

Not how I compare to so and so
Or how I measure up against this
expectation or that 'should'.

But how good I am at being me; at being my authentic, unique, utterly fabulous and flawed self.

I have decided to unlearn all the things that don't serve me.

Like listening to fear more than courage.

Fear boringly stops me from trying new things. So go away fear.

May I instead accept that I will fall over and make myself look silly when I try new things. Like babies when they first try to walk; oopsiedaisy.

But up they rise.

May I instead rise like baby me, with the courage to try, put one foot in front of the other.

And walk towards my dreams, boldly.

———

a prayer for the future

Whenever the wind grows cold and the trees are bare, let me remember the summer heat will reappear and the fruit will grow and I will again bask in the sunshine and pick summer fruits on lazy, hazy days.

To help with visualisation
I can see clearly in my mind's eye
The brightness of my future
The gladness of my dreams come true.

They stretch onward and upward
Over hilltops and mountains
As I reach for the sky
And the stars and the moon.

There are no limits to what I can achieve
And in these big dreams I do believe.

———

a prayer
of devotion

I take full responsibility for what and whom I devote my heart to, and where my motion towards my devotion takes me.

———

an affirmation
for courage

I invite my fear to dance with me.

We'll foxtrot across the dance floor
And shimmy across the sand
And skate and swirl across icy ponds.

The cracks in the frozen water may appear
But I shall not fall.

Instead I will step onto the crisp white snow
Knowing with certainty where I need to go.

Onward.

------

a blessing for growing and learning

May I remember that I am always learning
And may I stay open to new knowledge.

Every day I learn.

May I remember not to berate myself for
that which I don't yet know.

Most days I move forward, sometimes I
fall back
But mostly I progress onward.

Every day I grow.

May I remember to meet myself where
I am and honour me as I am today.

Every day I learn.

May I remember to be proud of myself.

―――――

a prayer for
persistence

May I try and be open to failing
Instead of simply not trying
Or stopping instead of persisting.

Let me learn from it all
These teaching tools
So I may keep on growing.

―――――

an affirmation about dreams

Things may not turn out exactly like I hope.

Things may be different to how I
imagine them.

Sometimes they'll be better
Other times they'll be worse.

Whether I'm excited or frustrated, I know
That everything truly counts.

_____

a blessing
on uncertainty

May I see uncertainty differently to the
way it is often feared
As something with endless possibilities.

I no longer need to run away from
uncertainty for I know it is part of life.

Uncertainty means I get to live with
possibility
And potential
And hope.

What a gift.

———

an affirmation
for change

I can wander from the path
I can pivot from the plan

I can take a break from the work
I can change direction
I am in control.

And it feels great.

———

on embracing change

Okay change
Let's do this.

It probably won't hurt
Not like I imagine.

More like seedlings out of dirt
And if I water the new seedling
And show it loving care
The seeds of change
Will take me far further than I thought.

And then in time I will look back
On what I thought was scary

And I will smile as I never imagined
The wonder of such beauty.

_____

a blessing for
self-belief

I am better than I think
And stronger than I know.

I can do difficult things.

So I have decided to abide by
the yaysayers
Ignore the naysayers.

And believe in myself and my dreams.

_____

a poem for
self-belief

I see you
And I see your spark
And your warm heart
And your kind remarks.

I see those glimmers of hope that shine strong
And I see magic in your future
And I know I'm not wrong.

I see you struggling to believe this truth
But I have faith in you and know you have
faith too.

When you look deep inside to that child
you once were
You know you can do this.

Yes, I see that spark.

_____

acceptance of the past

a prayer to accept what has been

My mistakes teach me.

My regrets guide me.

I need not be afraid of things going wrong
For all of my failures, mistakes and regrets
Lead towards doing things right next time.

They are signposts that guide me towards
my own betterment.

I need not be afraid of things going wrong
For they are a gift to my future self.

―――――

a blessing for everything

Everything counts.

The bad and sad moments count by showing me what I need to change.

The good and happy moments count by showing me what matters most.

The mistakes I make show me what not to do next time.

The successes I achieve show me I am capable.

Now that I know that everything counts I can rest into the peaceful serenity of that knowledge.

For nothing is perfect and everything is perfect and everything in life is my teacher.

———

a blessing
on failing

Getting things wrong is a gift.

Nobody gets things right all the time
That's something I will not forget.

No mistakes means I will not learn.

Without failure I cannot succeed.

Those lessons of mine
I've learned over time
Give value to how I proceed.

There is gold in the errors I've made
More precious than winning gold medals.

Bad choices and sad feelings offer reward
and direction by giving me signals.

———

enjoying
the present

a prayer
for play

May I have ice cream for breakfast every
once in a while
And dance around the kitchen.

May I twinkle with childlike playfulness
And remember who I am.

My sense of fun growing with me as I age.

———

help for
enjoying now

I've just woken up, yet already it's bedtime.

The week has just begun and yet it's
the weekend.

The other day I sat in my classroom,
looking out of the window.

But now here I am, much older than then.

Time has passed, experiences have
been lived
But how much has been savoured and
valued and cherished?

It is time to savour and value and cherish
It is time to enjoy today.

To make the most of the remaining time
To do what matters most with who
matters most
To add sparkle and light and colour to
our days
To appreciate the ordinary and value the
little things
To do it now, rather than leave it 'til later
To enjoy this minute, rather than wait.

Before all of the time has passed.

Before now is gone.

Because now is still here.

Today is the day to cherish each moment
of life before it passes on.

_____

a prayer for stillness

May we sit silently
Quietly
With contented hearts
In stillness.

May we only whisper
So we can hear rather than break
The silence.

May we sit without speaking

Just knowing
Understanding
The true beauty of the world
And the world of beauty within us.

———

a prayer
for enjoying
the journey

As I travel toward my desired destination
Whenever I find myself blinkered
My focus pulled by its promise
May I put on the brakes
and come to a halt
So I may enjoy the journey more deeply
and slowly.

May I look around me and marvel at what
is there in this moment

The views
The progress
The experiences.

May I pause to reflect on
How I'm feeling
What I'm knowing
Where I've come from
And may I make regular stops to savour
the moments en route.

May I be content with close and near
With reaching rather than reached.

Let the joy come from trying and doing
Rather than completing and finishing.

Arrival is only part of the joy
For the journey is as important as where
I am going.

———

a learning prayer

When I feel disappointed
May I look for the lesson.

What does this teach me
About my passions?

---

an affirmation for doing what you love

I will remember to do what I enjoy doing.

I will do it for the enjoyment of doing not for winning.

I will try new things which I might love for the experience of trying, not for perfecting.

I will stay open to learning and do things
purely for the enjoyment of them
Not only to become successful at them.

———

a prayer for
flourishing

I choose to flourish rather than languish.

This life is precious, it's time to notice.

———

a prayer for acceptance and flow

Legs downstream
In this river called life.

My goal is to journey along the river from its source until it merges with the sea.

Along its course, the river has steep banks, strong currents and raging rapids.

These represent unchangeable situations, such as past regrets or other people's real or imagined opinions.

Clinging to reeds or struggling up the slippery bank is like holding on to the unchangeable; it gets me nowhere.

Yet when I let go and flow, I am free to rise and fall, to get things right or wrong; to learn from the past as I leave it behind and keep progressing onward.

With my legs downstream I can conserve my energy, so I may better cope with challenges, rather than waste energy trying to resist the natural flow of life.

I accept I cannot control all obstacles in life; I can only control my reaction to them.

Let me be flexible enough to ride with the current rather than resist it.

To face my legs downstream, so I may go with the flow of the river and let it guide me from resistance to acceptance; from frustration to compassion; from anger to calm.

Legs downstream. Accepting.

Navigating my way onward
Taking the most direct course towards calm.

Leaving the past behind and pointing towards my future.

May I accept there is no calm without some form of cooperation with the rapids of life.

And see calm acceptance as not about avoiding reality, but about honouring it.

As not about denying difficulty or avoiding action, but rising to challenges when I have the strength to do so.

Nor is calm acceptance about giving up
The river will still flow
Life will still go on however I respond.

May I calmly notice what's in my way from a vantage point of acceptance, balance and compassion.

May I change what I can, but let go of what I cannot alter.

May I make peace with my past so I can prevent it from disturbing my present.

May I point my legs downstream in this river called life
And enjoy life's journey from a scenic and serene place
And go with the flow, rather than frantically fight against life's inevitable current of twists and turns.

May I remember that rapids don't last for the whole river.

The bank will become lower and the water shallower.

I will be able to climb out or stand on the river bed and pause for a moment.

In this way acceptance can be my antidote to pressure, expectation and perfection.

A gentle, steady pathway towards inner peace.

———

a blessing for healing

There is no healing without feeling.

I can only heal if I let myself feel.

May I welcome the full spectrum of my emotions and lean into them freely.

May I choose expression over suppression
And let my feelings free me.

May I see my feelings as signals guiding me on what I might accept or change or do something about.

May I see my feelings as signposts to encourage action or acceptance.

Feeling them heals me.

_____

a permission prayer

May I give myself permission to meander;
to go with the flow, flexibly
Not always to go the direct route
but to wander with curiosity
To wander and to wonder and to follow
those wonders wherever they may go.

It's okay to drift.

_____

a healing prayer

As I open the gates allowing emotions
to flow
May my feelings bring me healing.

After the rain whips and cleanses the
painful path
May sunlight shine in through my wounded
heart.

After clenched fists and jaws of the
toughest times
May love balm my bruises.

In between hostility and harmony
May time mend broken bridges
And as the rivers of hope ebb and flow
May the warmth of kindness replenish
my soul.

———

a prayer for rejuvenation

May I be pulled rather than pushed
Towards what matters most.

May I notice the small wins
And celebrate them properly.

May I ask for help when I need it
Without fear of judgement.

May I let go of what doesn't serve me
In service of myself.

May I spend time in the solace of solitude
So I may escape and process my day.

This is my prayer for rejuvenation.

———

a prayer for energy

When I feel myself slumping
My energy drained
I'll pick myself up and get myself outside
To bathe in fresh air and forest and light
To revitalise and energise and fill myself up
with delight.

———

for help with self-care

Dear heart and body
May I remember to listen to you.

May I ask you each day what you need.

And may I provide what you require
To always feel nourished and held.

———

a question about priorities

Where shall I place my energy today?

———

our
world

a house blessing

Thank you for my home.

May I always be thankful for
The roof over my head
The comfort of a sofa on which to sit
A nourishing kitchen in which to cook.

However humble or empty
Home is a place where I can retreat
Recharge and hibernate.

May I always be grateful for this place.

_____

a prayer for nature

Being among trees is where I want to be.

May I savour these moments of being held in the bosom of Mother Nature.

May I cherish each moment outdoors
Watching leaves spiral and dance as
they fall.

May I remember to stop, look up and
breathe deeply
To take in those rich scents of earth and
damp wood
To look up at the blue-grey sky through a
kaleidoscope of branches
To touch green moss and marvel at its
colours and texture.

May nature heal me.

May I listen to nature's sounds and heed its call to adventure.

May I tune in to the singsong birds and marvel at them in flight overhead.

May I accept nature's invitation to stay a little longer.

May I bow to the magnificence of trees as I stand shaded underneath their boughs.

May I never shy away from hugging a tree and telling them how much they mean to me.

May I stroll slowly through woodland and skip through fields and notice with curiosity the raindrop on the petal, the deepness of the berry and the texture of the leaf.

Thank you Mother Nature for all that you share.

When I'm with you I know all is well.

———

self

a blessing
for balance

May I balance striving for what I want with appreciation for what I already have.

May I balance taking care of others with taking care of myself.

May I balance screen time with green time, comfort with adventure and solitude with connection.

May I balance busyness with stillness, doing what I have to with doing what matters most.

May I balance being purposeful with meandering aimlessly
With gratitude for living a balanced life.

———

an authenticity affirmation

Being me is brave and bold.

Being who others say I should isn't.

May I remove any shackles that restrict me
In being my true authentic self.

My worth is not determined by others
It's determined by how me I am
And how unique.

And that is enough.

_____

an acceptance prayer

May I find peace in acceptance.

May I be willing to accept every inch of me

To trust I am where I'm meant to be
To learn to become the best of me.

May my mind be filled with love and
compassion for the not-always-easy
journey I've been on.

May I always remain open to learning
Accepting of what has already been
Hopeful about all that is yet to come.

———

an imperfection prayer

Sometimes I won't believe in
myself enough
But that's okay.

Sometimes I won't feel like doing what I
started to do
And that's okay.

Sometimes I'll say things I regret and do things badly and get things wrong
That's okay too.

Because that is what it means to be human, to be real
Because that is normal and something we all do.

So I give myself permission to be human
I permit myself to be imperfect.

And oh, how freeing that is.

———

a prayer for freedom

Today may I release the rules
The shackles of should
The rigid limitations
May I, for today, throw out the rule book

And do as I please with no responsibility.

May I taste the freedom
Of me, just being
Of just being me
To do as I please
To lead not to follow
Until I feel
Like I can again.

Healthy and ready .

———

a blessing for compassion

I often do not realise
Quite how beautiful I am
Nor how much I have to give
Nor how much I am given.

I sometimes lose sight
Of the gifts bestowed on me
Of the opportunities and possibilities
Of the wonder of my unique story.

But today, may I see my beauty
And receive my gifts
And give my love
To myself as much as I give to others.

———

a blessing on strength and vulnerability

Strong back (my ancestors stand behind me).

Soft front (I am open to giving and receiving love).

Wild heart (I feel all my emotions and care deeply).

Strong back (I am brave).

Soft front (I am loving).

Wild heart (I am passionate).

———

a prayer for compassion

May I honour myself and others
With the benefit of the doubt.

May I let us off the hook
With a permission slip
To mess up and fall down
To make mistakes
To remove blame and shame.

And replace them with love.

———

for help letting go

May I remember
It matters not what I think people think of me
For they are not thinking of me at all
They are thinking about what I think of them.

That's the loop that we live in.

Letting go frees us to be our own person.

———

an affirmation for self-love

Today I choose to replace criticism
with compassion
Discouragement with encouragement
Fretting with flourishing
And fear with hope.

———

a blessing for aging

Who's that looking back at me from that mirror on the wall? She looks a little older and wrinklier and grey.

But she also has experience and wisdom and warmth.

A calm acceptance, a freedom to be just who she truly is.

She doesn't have as much baggage as she did when she was young.

She's let go of perfection and expectation, although it took a long while.

She's stepped out of the shackles of should which had bound her with limitations.

She's bold and free and knows who she is, and I'm happy that she's me.

———

an affirmation of self-respect

I am not a burden
I am loved more than I realise.

I am enough
And I am here.

I honour this life
And I respect myself.

And I'm doing what I can
And that's enough.

I'm enough
And here I am

Living.

———